TAKING APART
THE BIRD TRAP

By the same author:

The Inheritors (2021)
The Silences (chapbook, with Robbie Coburn, 2016)
2012 and other poems (2012)

TAKING APART
THE BIRD TRAP

AMANDA ANASTASI

RECENT
WORK
PRESS

Taking Apart the Bird Trap
Recent Work Press
Canberra, Australia

Copyright © Amanda Anastasi, 2024

ISBN: 9780645973280 (paperback)

A catalogue record for this
book is available from the
National Library of Australia

NATIONAL
LIBRARY
OF AUSTRALIA

Cover image: 'silhouette of beautiful girl with birds, double exposure'
                by Designega
Cover design: Recent Work Press
Set by Recent Work Press
Author image by Nicholas Walton-Healey

recentworkpress.com

For my father, Paul.

Contents

I

II

III

IV

V

I

Afterlife

While you were here, you said twice:
When I am gone, there will be nothing.

It will be as if I am asleep; firmly uttered
as all the fibs and half-truths you told.

When I gave word for your breath's end
after explanations from careful nurses

waiting for me to break, it was strange
to see schedules and traffic continue,

each season yet slip into another, winter
easing and every Spring the first, second,

soon the third to happen after you. Benign
friends said *Look for signs from him.* I'd explain

your contempt for talk of angels and spirits,
the concept of heaven or the dead watching

over the living; how you'd scoff at bended knee,
at those professing to see Jesus in burnt toast

or tears from a statue's eyes. *It's the uneducated
that see it,* you'd say, and smirk at Italian widows

in their black shoes muttering chants at rosary
long memorised; funerals espousing a local man

as the perfect father, husband. *They knew he was a bastard,*
you'd quip. I'd say to friends, *If he is leaving me a sign,*

he's doing it against his will. It is now that I'm closer
to you; every aspect of your face feeling a mere

centimetre from mine. I hear your accent's coil
each time I seek it; tell one story after another

to keep you here. I hold a belief in the certain
ghost of memory and the afterlife of the page.

Collision

I imagine the last thing you saw
was your unforgiven father's face:
blank yet sneering, finally greeted
without rage. And the last contact
made by the fingers I once clasped,
the surface of a stranger's car hood
in a dull colour you could not abide.
You may have caught a myna bird's
call, dreamt of Venice or old Valletta
or a woman with flowers in her hair
or your big-eyed child tripping over
her own feet to get to you upon your
arrival home. Perhaps the last words
formed when being flung like litter
by a startled hoon in a haze of glass,
broken English and exhaust fumes:
Amanda. Dad here. I need your help.
I remember what it was
I wanted to tell you—

Monostich I: It Begins

I will never forget your locked presence.

When two things are said, there are ten unsaid.

Every day, we trust someone to stay within the lines.

I keep running into myself, veiled.

With you, an untold injustice goes.

Try looking up when the sky has been removed.

I have shown myself in quarters.

When all has been taken, rules are obsolete.

I closed a door that kept clicking open.

With each loss, a new eye blinks open.

Two Weeks After It Happened

The Bedsit

His belongings lay as if he had every intention of returning. Finger-smudged reading glasses on the kitchen counter on a layer of crumbs beside Dumas, Thich Nhat Hanh, Dawkins. The clearing of all traces of a man's existence from a room. I began my long, solitary work. The dust kept the one closest to me from helping. Friends and family were not asked. I didn't want them seeing the smoke-stained walls.

The Ladies

I sat with the funeral director who knew dad from lodge. We were filling out the form for the death certificate and I was struck by all the details I had to double check about his first family. When asked if I wanted a male or female celebrant, we said in unison, *Female. Paul liked the ladies.* I recalled the story dad told of when he first saw my green-eyed, long-legged mother walk into the office. *Hire her or I'll leave.*

Crossing the Road

In the police interview, they asked what dad usually crossed the road for. *Cigarettes and bread rolls.* I spoke of his frequent jaywalking and lack of patience for crossings; how he was slow on his feet; that I had warned him of the danger. They informed me of the CCTV footage held by the restaurant across the road.

I was afraid of what would happen to me if I viewed it, just as I feared what would happen if I witnessed the nurse removing his breathing tube.

The Fridge Notes

I compiled a box of his belongings to keep: used and new paint brushes, his rings, the remaining photos, large-lettered instructions I wrote for him on how to use the TV/DVD player for seniors. Notes I put on the fridge: reminders when to take his meds and one in bold black marker reading *If you need to tell Amanda something, write it down.* In his scratchy writing, his very last note on a scrap piece of paper: *Amanda will come at 3.30ish.*

Sniffing Paintings

I stood at the screen door while visiting, holding it ajar for air. He'd watch, amused. Languidly put out his cigarette. Five minutes later, I'd enter the flat though remain near the open door. Now, I search for the cigarette stench I abhorred, hoping a little of it will stay lodged in the canvases of his paintings and inside his books. The smell has now faded, though not gone. I sometimes detect it in the room without seeking it. Arriving, then passing.

Monostich II: Reversals

The trees in Siberia lay their heads to the ground.

The calendar is still set to last July.

The lost child is not crying.

I, the pupil in the eye of crisis.

The water has taken down the bridge.

The departure is the entrance.

The stranger becomes the brother.

Today, train tracks twist into roller coasters.

No Through Road: a challenge.

This poem is reading me.

Night Light

It is three weeks since you've passed. I am hearing
a creak at the end of my bed as if someone is sitting,

checking in. I turn my lamp on to see it is not the cat.
There are times in the very early hours when I forget

this is the fifth room I have occupied. I am waking
to the first room with the walls you painted lilac,

mum striding the hall on the other side of my door,
the overflow of your coffee percolator on the stove,

the click of the boots that you wear to appear taller.
I run to their sound on tiles upon your arrival home.

Bedtime: you rapidly chalk a cartoon on my room's
little blackboard of a scene from a film just chuckled

over or a neighbourhood story mum is remarking on
between her habitual humming of old pop love tunes.

I fall asleep giggling: a gift no parent gave the child
version of you. I wish to have been alive back then

to rattle an impersonation or an absurd story; tell it
as if it were real. Watch your face learn early to smile.

An Apology

It was always enough. The amplification of crickets calling from the roots of your hydrangeas during sundown. The clear night air carved with a streak of nicotine and hushed storytelling. The post-flood creek inching ever closer to our fence when the rain dropped and persisted, the water's brown coat smoother than any eighties plastic surface. Your dusk garden escape from arguments. Your arms that I'd hang from made of war and slipshod, back-handed parents, bitter marriages and ships in foreign ports. Waiting for the cool change against our cheeks. It was always easier for you out here than in the crowded house that could not hold you. Years later, the late-night interruptions of your twenty-eight second phone calls were enough: your attempt at reaching out with no discussion. All the non-confessions were enough. The plastic flowers in your one-bedroom flat mimicking your once garden. The bird statues placed on your bookshelf instead of the rock walls caging your flower beds that you built delightedly and I would tease you about. You, smiling as I enter. Toward the end, you were content to be silent and not divulge, though I wished you would. There were many questions you did not answer and so many I did not ask. Yet, it was so much more than enough.

II

Scratches

Biro marks, instantly recognisable;
intended to be barely legible.

The same feathered bars used in Santa's
decorative letters punctuated with lively

drawings of bells, flowers and deer,
congratulations on my good grades

and a warning to not *fall off the bridge*—
your metaphor for teenage waywardness.

The same hand on essays I was tasked
with typing on free thinking and the dangers

of blind faith. The very hand notating names
and numbers on paper scraps—misplaced,

uncategorized—of clients and old friends;
one by one, each becoming a stranger again.

In later years, room appeared between
the pen strokes like the parts of a barbed

wire fence pushed out to form a thin
corridor, though never quite wide

enough for the full story to show itself
or to overcome a lifetime of camouflage.

Ask No Questions

My parents' wedding photo:
the smallest on the mantel,

crammed in a ceramic frame
larger than the picture itself;

sitting among other family
snapshots: crooked, tense,

like a mouth lying by omission
or a two-word answer.

It was cut from a group photo
to accommodate the chosen,

tiny frame. They pose charmingly
in the wedding ceremony gardens.

She is wearing a brimmed hat
in lieu of a veil. He is in a suit

with shirt frills. The guest list
seems to be select and small.

There are things about that day;
before, during and after it I still

do not know. In this house, details
are extracted only when altogether

necessary. Mum has recommended
my wedding and choices be different

though rolls her eyes at written vows,
retreats from my questions, steps away

from commentary. Like an infinitely
held up passenger, I crave movement.

Growing Up Near the Blow Ups

Formerly ICI, Deer Park

We never set eyes on it when being driven
by mothers who dug their polished nails

into steering wheels, shushing kids with Maccas
toys in the back seat. It was a well-known secret,

both carried and kept by the locals. Dense
tree barriers stood between the explosives

facility and the edge of the Western Highway.
Not a sound emanated from such a distance

or from the noisy hallways of the suburb's
homes, well-shielded by '70s brick, lengthy

gardens with sprinklers and smooth nature strips.
A schoolmate called the place a dynamite factory.

Our nearest neighbour called it Old Blowups
and spoke of how, decades ago, workers died

in accidental explosions adding *No accidents happen
now*. Then, once again, we would forget it was there.

Years later, the local paper reported that a remotely
controlled bulldozer had cleared the site of chemicals,

though experts said *nitro glycerine* could stay undetonated
in the soil for years. Sites were rezoned, some deemed

far enough to not be contaminated; carved up
for residential house and land packages, sold

by tight-lipped local real estate agents who knew,
like we all did, that not all pasts can stay buried

and will surface eventually like tense, dormant
marriages, unnamed slights; like neglect mixed

with nurturing; as gatherings and party dresses
cannot entirely remove the likelihood of little

explosions occurring. Although, often, small joys
sprout like obstinate daisies between the cracks.

The Gift in the Dirt

For the Growling Grass Frog—currently endangered

I shape my hands into
a tender enclosure, thumbs
light on its braille-like back.

A small inspection begins
between the ramshackle
walls of my palms:

a preparation to bolt.
The constraint unlocks.
I watch the quick work

of delicate legs readying
for the leap—they recoil,
propel as an archer's bow.

I still feel its tiny feet pushing
against my skin, springing up
and onward in a split second:

my first reminder that the will
for swift travel is innate
and escape always possible.

Backyard Camping

On Christmas Eve, a tent was pitched
between the washing line and rock garden.

The backyard became a campground.
Dad started a small (definitely illegal) fire

with his cigarette lighter to boil a billy.
I'd roast pink marshmallows bought

from the milk bar. *Who needs to drive to the bush
when we have this?* he'd say. *Who wants to hear a story?*

I sat to attention as he began a tale made more
compelling by the slow ease of its telling—

every line a hook. Often the main character
was a frog—namely, a misfit red frog, teased

by the other frogs though unbothered by it.
Other tales featured an adventurer, Pasquale,

who napped under a sombrero between prank
playing on local villagers, hitching rides on trains

where the destination was unknown; always faring
well in the end. I hung on every line as the story

unfolded, aware that my response was feeding
the narrative's direction like a *Choose Your Own*

Adventure book. I awaited the next makeshift tale:
a portal that I was not alone in escaping through.

Suburban Deer

Mediterranean columns against brown brick. Kids squabble
about whose turn it is to hide in their game. Careful gardens.

Pebbled strips A terracotta skinned girl carrying colour
pencils in a Barbie case, skipping past the cream, closed

lids of roller shutters. Low powerlines. A disruption
of gumtrees. The slanted, round scribbles of thirteen-

year-old romance on the bus stop. A cross atop plain brick,
interrupted by stained glass. An unspoken grudge. A lined,

slow-moving lady in black clutches her Sunday missal
and envelope of coins, a whiff of provolone and bleach

on her fingers. Neat, creased shoes Broken glass. Holding
a rosary, the parishioner spits on the steps. Old men gather

like seagulls at the shopping centre bench, shirking their wives'
gossip and wiped down kitchens. They talk of the rising price

of fruit and the replacement of the parish priest. A measured
greeting at the crossing. Flowers tied to a pole. Twitchy kids

leave their marks using souped up cars like paint brushes,
in the earliest part of the morning when the roads are clear.

Monostich III: Blocks

Your face is a half-closed shutter.

The cat reacts to a presence I cannot see.

Something unseen reacts to the cat.

The guests have not departed.

A hoarder is one who rejects the present.

Your reply is your unopened hand.

The bird exits one trap to enter another.

The primary witness is not looking.

The mountain lion is on a leash.

I falter at the last door.

The Chair in the Fig Tree

While tending to his fruit trees and aviary of finches,
I sat in the fig tree where two thick boughs diverged.

His garden of ivies and statues lightly held me.
I gazed over the fence beyond the wild gums

of Kororoit Creek. One day, a red plastic chair
appeared in the tree where I sat, its legs wired

to the branches. *You sit there all the time. I thought
to make it comfortable for you.* Barely containing

my bafflement, I thanked him, attempted to sit
in the tree chair, found it impeded my ability

to clamber up, to turn, to alter my vantage point.
Often, I told him when his garden endeavours

extended to the over-zealous: when he sawed off
the back of an old chair, nailed it to the fence

and proclaimed *This is art!* Or when he cemented
yet another gnome atop the rock wall or painted

the driveway in left-over paint, whatever the colour.
Weeks went by without tree climbing. He removed

the chair without a word and we were back to how
we were. I, dreaming of distant places and people

I would one day meet, and he tending to flowers
(more suited to the climate and soils of Europe)

and his zebra finches—chirping, rich in colour.
Hopping about in airy, well-furnished cages.

Child of the Creek Speculates

Kororoit Creek, Deer Park

How many trees does it take to ward off
the metallic dust from shopfronts, street

sign poles and the wearing of tyres, exhaust
fumes of the roadway; front lawn pesticides

and over-fertilised turf of new housing estates
where old gums are pulled out to be replaced

by saplings held by sticks and plastic tree guards,
woven among neat footpaths for prams and power

walkers in lycra? How many thousand-year-old
river red gums does it take to cancel the sweep

and screech of highway; the site of slow walking
to school, daily jibes and teens smashing up cars

to sad/derisive commentary of parents (not the ones
weeping on the news for their lost *good boy* sons)?

How much runoff from rooves, drains and driveway
car washes until, bit by bit, it lodges in the waterway?

How long until the algae on the water's surface collects
to the point of forming a magnificent yet toxic bloom

for locals to gaze upon; to ask where the ducks, herons
and yabby fishers are and where the children now play?

The Piano Eisteddfod

An audience of fidgeting children,
half listening, half readying to play
on a vast stage to a six-year-old eye.
I begin the gruelling deviation
from my daily practice. First,
a mistake in opening quavers.
Then, a fudged chord. I keep
playing as I'd been instructed.
I bow, as told, before returning
to my mother—unimpressed.
You don't have to play the next
if you don't want to. We can go.
I am unmoved, as if fearing
to disturb the ready dynamite
her words had just lit in me.
We can go home if you want.
I wait my turn to then make
my second, steady approach
to the polished beast. This time
it is a character piece (Hutchens'
Evening), every note striking
the perfect balance between
softness and clear *cantabile,*
the left-hand wave-like
beneath. After the final
ritenuto, I bow resolutely.
I note her altered face.
I skip past her appraisal.
I am ready to go home.

Playing Detectives

I started a game on weekend afternoons with my brother:
Let's play detectives. You spy on mum. I'll hide in the garden and watch dad.

Dad would be where I expected him to be like an old fruit tree,
silent except for the sound of watering. The air smelled of basil,

jasmine and the opening of a story. Each of his flowers flourished.
Soon, he'd move to the undercover garden and I'd sit on the ledge

that encircled it. He'd say with surety, *You're a special breed, Eleanor,*
sticking to the name he chose at my birth. He'd mimic a neighbour

to make me giggle: Georgina shrieking in Greek for her husband
to come inside or Little David who'd holler for my brother until

he emerged. His accent curled around his words like a hand hold.
She never listens, he'd often say. I would ask why he married her.

I'd ask her the same. He'd talk of his six-year-old self, *Little Paolo*
who'd get into trouble for questioning the Sunday school teacher.

How his first years were *running from one air raid shelter to another.*
How he'd save his coins to sneak off to the cinema to see Bogart

and Bergman. How priests ran the village, how you could not say
a word against them; how he swiftly left the island for the Navy.

Then one time, motioning to the house: *She never asked why I am*
the way I am, his eyes narrowing to the closest expression to hurt

he'd allow himself. Beneath his words and watering, black crickets
began their chorus. He cut the quiet so slightly yet surely,

he was almost at one with it. Our notes from the detective game
were brief. A mention of mum humming an indecipherable tune

over the kitchen sink and dad giving his petunias, daffodils
and geraniums all the tenderness he was afraid to give to her.

First Protest

We were protesting against the build
of a proposed incinerator, considered
by some to be too close to residents.

I made signs out of old cardboard with slogans like
No to pollution and *Our children need to breathe clean air.*

On the day of the protest, I slid glances at my father
handing out the *How to Vote* flyers I had helped him
fold all morning. He was wearing a slick grey suit

in his suave style of semi-activism. Across the afternoon,
I listened as he uttered the same lines to different people.

Upon the arrival of the local paper's photographer,
dad handed my brother one of my signs to pose with
reading, *No incinerator in our backyard!*

A week later, the photo of a forlorn dark-haired boy
holding up a sign surrounded by disgruntled locals

(with frequent mention of my dad's local election
campaign) were strewn across page two.

Years later, I asked dad if they'd built
the incinerator. He replied through
cigarette smoke *Of course they did.*

They were always going to build it.
Did you really think any different?

The Broken Bird Trap

He'd set the trap, load it up,
sit at the other end of the yard
and wait. Tell us to hush; revel
at the snap of the trap shutting,
check to see if what we'd caught
was a goldfinch or a sparrow.

He'd kneel and gaze, point
at its black and yellow wings,
its mask of deep red indicating
it was male. I'd watch the bird
hop about, attempting to make
sense of the barrier hindering it.

I opened the trap one afternoon,
smashed it with a rock and threw
each busted part over the fence.
Dad gaped, too impressed to be
cross. He had never responded
to my protests with anger,

content to see dissension rise
in me. He'd make an irreverent
or racist remark and watch me,
yet again, rebuke him strongly.
He would smile as he studied
my reaction to his latest test.

Wordless, he'd set a new trap in place
of the old; continuing the entrapment,
the observation, the tying of a ribbon
to a goldfinch's leg before letting it fly.
He'd hold the bird in his leathery hand;
feel the weight of a thing about to be free.

Wing

At the beginning of outstretch,
there is a contraction from the keel.

An anchorage in the breast.
Lift is created by altering air.

The central vane hits the wind
and the upstroke for the thrust.

The only posture is that of crucifixion
in a glisten of black and blue and red.

The open-mouthed dependency
of the bristling nest is far behind.

There are many destinations.
The sky is the resting place.

Monostich IV: Sightings

Anything I say will be used for the show.

Every wall has an aperture.

You are the artist who paints what he hasn't seen.

My imaginary friend is now visible to all.

I sweep niceties under the carpet.

Sun is pleasant only for a time.

I swim in a pool while I dream of the sea.

She visits strangers because they are family.

I return to the discomfort of home.

The page turner is too conspicuous.

Trust only the unfamiliar.

Seek liberation without curbing another's.

The student retreats from the difficult passage.

The untelling is your mistake.

Mismatch

She glances at me warily
as if perusing a foreign land
she had not been prepared

to visit and feeling too out
of place to leave the hotel
and explore the foreshore;

remarking on the furnishings
and decor to avoid discussing
what waits beyond the room

or beyond the transaction
held with her own mother:
a self-shaping arrangement,

a compliance to the point
of puppetry; a perpetual
unease with independence.

When I gaze into the hesitant
sea of her eyes as she speaks,
startled by their beauty: a green

I'd only seen in atlases
to denote elevations, I hunt
for a point of kinship. When I try

to dive in, I fall out the other side,
though I will always circle around
and try again, looking for a raft.

Good Shoulders

The closest thing to a hug I received from my father
was a slap on the shoulder as if I were a prize horse.

Good shoulders, he'd say to the kid he'd selected to realise
his unfulfilled ambitions in art, politics, general human

relations and English language mastery. A long-running
joke was to take an ordinary sentence and re-phrase it

by using unnecessarily long words. *I am going to the supermarket*
became *I am now journeying to the establishment from whence I will*

purchase some produce. Each time, we laughed at my excessive
phrasing and each time, when I read out Wilde or Shakespeare

(after his retort of *Instead of 'Listen' he says 'Lend me your ears'!*),
he'd smile. I soon could see that I was merely a participator

in his delusion that he could not be all he wanted to be;
that the child would write it, articulate it better than he.

And so, he would say *Anyone can get married and have kids!* or
Go into politics! or *When are you going to write that book about...?*

So, when he saw me take my walks along the creek trail,
when the old women walking their husbands and dogs

would say *You're brave, walking here, a young woman alone,*
Dad would say, *There is a woman with a destination.*

III

Cinderella: A Retelling

Upon entry into the happily-ever-after,
there is the stamp of a bright stone,

an inhale between bone and steel housed
in cloth; the funambulist's skill of precise

performance for reliable, light applause.
The eyelets of the dress's back are laced

by the painted finger of another; a pastel-
hued waltz to a too familiar croon. It feels

like progression, from indifference to all
eyes toward. Father's ghost reappears in

the champagne. Mother's bubbles of chatter
sail without a word of sober congratulations.

If called upon to speak she could not define
the peculiarities of him beyond title. A dazed

laugh into the night as the first of the questions
sits and rotates. The gradual fall of the masks

of the evil and the good, of the frippery from
the substance, of the unknown to the known.

Child Free

They have stopped asking
if I will or won't and why

as though I were an incubator
delayed, or a worker on the edge

of falling in line to the expected agreement.
As each year arrives, it became less and less

enquired about: the odd choosing of no genetic
add-on, though I add hourly, daily and yearly

to my encounters, nurturings, functions, ever
evolving creations, elements of which remain.

I have stopped offering reasons. From dad: *Pfft!*
Pigeons breed! He understood my need to be free.

From mum, as though it were unquestionable creed:
You are not complete as a woman if you do not have a child.

I didn't reply. Just wondered who had said the words
to her; why she accepted them, repeated them to me.

Portrait of a Departing Lady

Funeral plans: a wall crypt underneath
her mother's; pink roses on the pew ends.

A house-size increase upon the exodus
of children, husband, friends, dissention.

Her disdain for the coverings of foreigners,
unusual hairstyles, childless women.

The mismatched furniture, each piece
never appearing to belong in the room.

The cupboards filled to the flimsy doors
with unused containers and forgotten dolls.

Her terror of the freeway; ringed fingers
clutching the steering wheel, a precipice.

Today, a relative's sixtieth. She fidgets
and retorts en route, wishing to be home.

I suggest revolt and a turning of the car.
She looks at me wide, an uncertain child.

Turning her head to avoid my curious eye,
she squeezes the wheel and continues.

Her lipstick: two red lines, ever-increasingly
not quite matching the shape of her mouth.

Monostich V: Departures

The bride's doubt is visible through the veil.

A string of weeds or a daisy chain?

A forest cannot be tended by a hand rake.

You have left yourself a thousand times.

This new blaze will not be suppressed.

The Scream

He halts as though a switch had been clicked
at the sound. Kneeling beside my curled up
body, he swiftly shapes himself into seeming
gentility. I envision remaining in this soft
minute, all harsh words fallen; witnessing
the finding of the point where the will
to be kind defeats the impulse to transfer
piled up self-loathing on the one in near
proximity. Slightly smirking:
      Shh. The neighbours will hear you.
I react as though I have sighted a door,
ajar, I had thought was locked beforehand
and not wanting him to know I had seen it.
I return to the refuge of quiet; neaten my face
to its usual state of expressionless in crisis.
Exit via the sliding door. Sit in the yard until
the daylight entirely fades to dusk. Decide
to not go back in. Choose to see openings
I now realise had always been there.
Now, to walk. To not be deterred.

Carrier of the Child

At lunch, my whole body was pointed
toward you like a bent yet certain arrow.

You could see there was something bereft
in me that day, but you didn't know how

to broach or hold it. We remained, as we
always did, on the periphery of each other;

the carrier of the child confused as she
looked down at the bundle in her arms—

only increasing as the child grew, began to speak
and form contrary ideas, viewpoints, ways to live

in the world. I understand that I am a puzzling
outcome, but you must know our time is nearly

up. I will always be pointing toward you, scratching
at the door, sticking my fingers between the shutters.

Is there anything you need to tell me? I will always
slide a glance at you. There is still time. I wait.

IV

Inside the Apartment

A bird trap set with a shaky wire, where his heart
should be, that catches purple, red, yellow-plumed
birds that fly out and in again. A terrestrial globe
acquired from a local store, placed on a small table
with a leg about to give way. A six-foot cupboard
piled with lies that never got in the way of a story,
old flight tickets, re-watched cowboy films. An empty
shelf at the bottom where dust spells out, in capital
letters, the names of the people he was careless with.

A painting by his hand of a woman resembling me,
clothed in head-to-toe white, staring into the ocean
with five white birds flying in the distance. It covers
the whole wall. He, leaning over a kitchen counter
coated in layers of cigarette ash. I, fidgeting smilingly
and colouring the silence. *Do you have anything to tell me?*
I leave space for an answer, but he cannot find words.
Except once. *I see parents with their kids now. I wish
I had shown you more affection when you were young.*

Another time: *I hated my father.* I talked about forgiveness.
No words, though he seemed to listen. I retrieved my phone
and scrolled the Birds of Australia Insta page. Every corner
of his face changed. *Pink Robin, Rainbow Lorikeet.* Remember
our aviary, I said. The canaries you turned bright orange.
My eyes seeking one of your stories, as purple geraniums
enveloped me. The garden with forgotten coffee spoons
behind the fixed grins of gnomes. A goldfinch with a red
ribbon tied to its leg, trapped and freed by the same hand.

Monostich VI: Curiosities

Inside the cage, another cage.

Our halted conversations haunt me.

There are hajla marks in the ash.

The seams of your smile are fraying.

I gathered myself too fast.

You half arrived and never landed.

I can still get to you despite your locks.

I mourn in brightest colour.

The answer is in your question.

There was a day I forgot to be cautious.

I cannot walk away from a curious mind.

The child in me asks.

The Missing

These days, it does not happen upon the sight
of oranges or halva on the supermarket shelf
or when I walk past the café table where we sat
with coffee and sandwiches after your brain scan.
Or when I obscure myself among your plants outside
our old house, now with other people moving around
inside it who, surely by now, have seen me wrapping
my hands around their pink geraniums and bottlebrush.
It happens, now, when I return home from being unseen
or mistaken, when the room I am inhabiting is strangely
bare of a dry, impudent or short-sighted remark,
when I have not yet experienced a belly-aching joke.
Then, there you are. Sitting in me like the limestone
in the La Pietra you were born near—sturdy, mulish,
silent but listening; a rough-hewn, quite failed, absurd
version of everything I've ever wanted in a person.

Calling

It is not that I expect
my call to be answered
or to hear his voice in
greeting. It is the brief
moment to enact a once
daily task: to seek his name
on my contact list and dial
before *This number has been
disconnected* sounds. Twelve
undeleted voice messages
sit like holsters in my inbox.
Each one, the same: *It's dad.
Call me when you get some time.*
Only one has an addendum,
playfully said: *You are a hard
woman to reach.* The number
will stay listed until the day
my phone is dead. His key
will stay hooked to my chain
as if, once again, I am visiting
the last neglected room strewn
with unessentials he called home.

The Last Visitor

July 2022

The accident: captured on the CCTV
of a Chinese take away. Approximately
2 P.M. on a bright winter Saturday.

Multiple witnesses. Ambulance arrival
in minutes. A call is received from the Royal
Melbourne and a policeman with a sensible

Anglo name speaks to the man's next of kin:
a daughter who doesn't answer the first call.
Incident described on the evening news as:

An 82-year-old pedestrian hit by a car in Melbourne's
outer west is in critical condition. Other story of the day:
Record heatwave makes its way across Europe.

The daughter would have fixated on the images
of Parisians sweltering and splashing in fountains.
Perhaps noted the fatalities due to extreme heat.

Today her mind is filled with one simple
unkempt man who sneered at *God,* said
that the only love that exists is between

a parent and child; who locals thanked for his deeds.
Described by ex-wives as dishonest, ill-tempered.
Just one child still contacts and sees him:

his last visitor. There is an unexpected though familiar knock at the door. He is handed a bag of nuts and fruit. On this day, his eyes betray joy. Witnessed by one.

Monostich VII: The Floods

In response to the 2022 NSW Floods

He begins to cross a sinking bridge.

A horse, almost submerged, halts.

A mouse clings to a swimming snake.

A cow is motionless on the swaying roof.

The river swallows a boat, still peopled.

Ways I Said I Love You Without Saying I Love You

There was a cleaning frenzy in your flat. A sorting and returning of books to your almost bare shelves. The neat placing of pencils and brushes in a mug so you could sit at your desk again. There was a portion of leftover lasagne kept in my freezer until I next saw you. I'd never stick to the shopping list you gave me, adding cashews and olives. Making phone calls for you and joking about the ear-violating waiting music while on hold. Telling you the bills were paid and all was well. Asking you how the kitchen got so filthy. Buying you a new calendar with orange and pink scenes of desert plains. Answering the same question you asked me last week about a California town you wanted to visit that you saw in a western once. Fetching you drawing pads and pencils and commissioning a sketch of a bowl of fruit during lockdown. Accompanying you to the GP; refuting your assertion that you were taking your medication daily. Locking eyes with you while the doctor gave you the lecture about what would happen if you didn't take the tablets. Guiding you to a seat in the socially distanced waiting room. Asking you to face me so I could fit your mask properly over your nose. The flood in my chest when you allowed me a tiny window into your inner world after returning from hospital: *Oh, it feels good to be home.* A close falling apple, I do not know how to form this emotion into a fitting, coherent response. Proceeding to organise your sink, I ask again with a shake in my voice *Is there something you want to tell me?*

Critiquing My Father's Art

Your technique was hit and miss. As I told you of Van Gogh —whose work you would not reconcile as *good art*—it was not about replication but feeling. Your painting was a snapshot from a dream: heightened depictions of a Venetian street filled with a romanticism that no one, least of all you, saw coming. It was the way you dreamed the world to be imposed on the way you saw it. You painted from memory and an imagination smirking. You did not sit before the landscape you depicted. The characters you painted did not sit before you: flawed of skin, fidgety, hiding pain. You'd often say, *Never tell or give all of yourself.* As always, I defied you daily in this, moving beyond safekeeping and refuting the half embrace. In the house we shared, I was clamouring for a new way between two people skimming the surface and burying parts of themselves. People who could no longer bear the lack of presence of the other but continuing. You were often wordless, concealing a realm within. As in the paintings, there was something boundless yet unrealised.

The Haunting

The ruthless highway of strangers passing quick.
Semitrailers sounding as though breaking apart.

Cars speeding above limit. You, moving slower
every day and not understanding the need,

even in your young years, people feel to rush
about; why I walk so very fast. You, lingering

as if you have endless time to spare, dissecting
each person passing. Arguing with the Jehovahs

while mum is looking on in disbelief at the window.
Gifting strangers with compliments or witty jibes.

Sitting me down for another story—your voice,
the magical sound of my young world. One story:

your arrival in Australia wearing a powder blue suit
and frilly shirt; the Aussies laughing and calling out

Look at that wog and *Ya poof!* We, laughing, falling
into prolonged silence as you continue your garden

watering. When you have no flowers to water,
you begin wilting until, one day, you are being

propelled like dandelion pappus. I, wondering if
it was an accident. Checking the witness statements.

Today, I am walking slower, frequenting the road's
empty benches. Haunting the places we once were.

Monostich VIII: The Reef

What displaces the fish displaces the mammal.

In glass-bottomed boats, tourists take selfies.

The cyclone flings a coral skeleton.

White coral. The tour boat accelerates.

Baby turtles rise to a new shore.

More fishing. The barbs of the starfish sharpen.

Coral breaks with the tap of a diver's fin.

Where the fish go, the seabirds follow.

The underwater graveyard is stirring.

Reef Tourist Boat

Cairns, Queensland, October 2022

While the marine biologist speaks
of the changed course of the water bird,
families are scrolling through holiday
snaps while others peel off wetsuits.

He leaves at the tour's end and I follow,
catching his stride as he disembarks
and heads to the Cairns foreshore:
You were the only one to mention climate change.
I tell him of my writing task at the reef.

His pace slows, his face becoming relaxed.
*I try not to mention it too much. People are here
on holiday and want to have fun. I know they
are not on the boat for a lecture on what is really
happening here, but I have to mention it ... at least once.*

As dusk falls, the esplanade begins to teem
with tourists, music blaring alongside birds
on tidal mudflats. I locate the section soon
to be buried in concrete. The egrets and terns
will find another place to live, and I will need
to carry my loss into another way of being.

A Short Summary of Fallen Birdsong

When coal miners brought canaries into the pit, forewarning workers of toxic air, helmeted men whistled to them while they worked. They would look up to locate them, alert to the soft fall of feathered bodies from the odourless gas. When Michigan's robins were wiped out from eating worms infected by chemically coated crops, a silent Spring without a dawn chorus was created. When pelicans ingested DDT-infested fish, every day it built in their sturdy yet delicate bodies. Though they lived, their eggs would be thin-shelled and break in their nests, unable to hold the weight of their young. When the Regent Honeyeater had no peer from which to learn their own song, they imitated the melodies of others, the bird's female counterpart now disinterested. From the first occurrences of migrating birds colliding with buildings to onlookers' dismay, birds have signed what is to come. Disappearing are the guiding markers counted on for decades and the places for rest along the way. We are surrounded by redirected and halted journeys, by missed cues and fallen songs.

An Option

There is no time
to board a vessel remaining still
at port, shifting only in reaction
to the movement of the waves;
merely imagining a new voyage.
Sitting before an advancing tide,
cracked open by new grief,
holding the fresh and awful
knowledge of transience,
I see what must be done.
I have arrived at the point
of envying the bold eye
of an empty-bellied gull;
the progress of moray eel,
of clown and cardinal fish
over coral, the astonished
face of the masked diver.
New voyage is an option:
at all times, in all places.
A revival of movement.
A newly paced step.
In less sculpted replies
and realms, I am going
to recognise myself.

The Version of Me That Didn't Leave

Silent. My hair is pulled back neatly.
I am cooking to the sounds of the tv
blaring on a channel set by another.
Earphones worn instead of requesting
the quiet I craved. Thinking something
I dare not say aloud. Not questioning
or disturbing the familiar ritual. Jokes
about the cat: the increasingly go-to
safe subject. I make a face; lighten
the mood the way mum did to relieve
her strained hallways. The laughter
is relieving for both of us. I return
to that refuge of silence. Consider
saying what needs to be said, rotate
the words in my mind to determine
a risk averse time/mode and version
of delivery. Consider if I will be able
to withstand the reaction if it comes.
The waiting to speak becomes untenable.
I carefully select between gentle or joking.
If the expected storm does not come,
I will exhale as though disembarking
a fairground ride. If it does, I'll turn
myself into a thing of steel: delayed,
non-reactive. I await my mother's
barbed wire eye glaring at me from
the face of another.

I am a woman who can fend for herself.
I am here because I love. I am committed.
I am content with my life as a whole.
I do not need more than this.

The Elephant

The elephant in the room lifts its pillar-like leg. Upon the sole of its foot is etched a diagram, detailing the myriad shocks and broken pieces that have kept it flourishing in the room. Upon its heavy skin are pages of slights accompanied by jokes, reused manipulations, half-baked conclusions, a resistance to challenge, obdurate routines that are somehow calming, vast stretches of absence, a circling around facts. There are wounds, broad and festering from neglect and inattention. The house it stands in has become less and less able to contain it, as the animal gets larger and increasingly comfortable. It has started foraging inside cupboards, haphazardly pulling out photo albums and keepsakes. Its trunk is precise enough to crack a nutshell and strong enough to lift and unplug an appliance and transport it to the opposite side of the room. It tries to wrestle with the incensed cat. There are veiny cracks appearing between the cornices and walls and above the fractured floorboards. The creature can now be heard by those passing by outside of the room. The elephant diminishes the presence of any person standing or weeping beside it.

Monostich IX: Realisations

Somewhere, a woman mutes her words.

Passivity is your greatest weapon.

I am striking a match over a black wick.

Your bags were always by the door, ready.

I make the intruder a drink.

I am not shivering from cold.

Now, I see the strings attached to my arms.

I love you—misdirected mail.

You are denied passage to the next chapter.

Repose arrived abruptly.

I seesaw between docile and rebellious.

The jungle is not out there.

V

Change of Play

When they close the playgrounds, the children will not miss
the slide and swing of fingers on painted metal. They'll meet
adventures waiting in the space they now find themselves.

When their screens die, they'll spin dizzily in lounge rooms,
part and twist rug fibres into skyscrapers, scarecrows or forests
of warriors fighting off brambles and perils in a strange land.

Their mothers almost smile, as their whole backyards convert
to rivers as the kids giggle and pretend they are some version
of *Swamp Thing*; float on the surface, mimic detached arctic ice.

Some will stick twigs in floating pots to make them sailboats,
setting out on a voyage on new waves; turn rubbish bin lids
into islands and car sunshades into shorelines. In a moment,

unwashed and their schedules strangely tilted; after a short sulk
at the unexpected departure, they will look about in fascination
at a changed world in our eyes but the only known world in theirs.

Write

At a desk, I unsling
a new truth, watch a worm
manufacture silk and simile,
enter the belly of a disoriented
earwig, bruise several niceties,
engineer twenty pedestrian
expressions to arrive at one
original line, admit and then
cast out the seventh angel;
cultivate a paper-thin self
consciousness. Work as if
falling into a steady slumber.
Sleep with one eye and hand
open, catching. Unearth abodes
well beyond these simple walls.
Once again, make warm cradles
out of chaos. Step back and stare
as the treasure room opens.

Landing

It is the solid landing, the lowering of wheels
to the outer layer of a place, beating with new

possibility rather than the acceleration and soar
at the starting of departure that causes the thrill.

It is the parting of clouds and the gradually
clearing view of desired ground; the journey

beyond the transportation; the waiting of wheels
to hit, decelerate and brake as an arm steadying

a tremor. It is a familiar anchoring, a welcome
retreat from the unnatural separation of flight;

the embrace of feet with ground. A returning
to human: the beautiful walking after hours

suspended between two places in a space
the body grudgingly inhabited. It is arrival.

Monostich X: Glimpses

The phone holds the man.

Art needs at least a small death.

Some goodbyes are a greeting to oneself.

I place a foot on shell-less ground.

There is a time for dropping calculations.

In the rubble, a swing set.

Keep your cards flying from your chest.

Your temperate retreat has changed me.

I do not accept your politeness.

Meet Me Here

Notice me in a room
when I am quiet to enter.

See a mirror, a contender
and a balm in my eyes.

Venture yet further from
a world you thought you knew.

Show me a face containing
both softness and edge.

Seek a singular journey
that part settles your yearning.

Locate the least entered door.
Instantly turn the handle.

Ask the question you are compelled to.
Be relentless in uncovering the answers.

Keep curiosity. Refuse to let it dim.
Be utterly certain in your uncertainty.

Become and remain daring
by admitting you do not know.

Cleanly articulate every feeling
even if your answer is delayed.

Seek meticulousness in discovery
of self and of others. Meet me here.

Lost Phone

There is a disorientation of hand and eye.
An attachment, seemingly vital, removed.

Not finding it is relinquishing the grip
of a handrail at spiral stairs. A curtain

begins to lift. I observe surrounding traffic.
I take in passing shapes, strides and faces,

habitually quizzical, downturned. The subtle
shifts of brow upon receiving a notification.

The absent stride of commuters arriving home,
still scrolling. I witness small openings between

shuffles by one another; between coffee orders
and tram stops, between phone checking ticket

queues and train loud talkers. Unintentionally,
I meet a rogue eye—it is mutually uneasy yet

pleasing. I note the precise slope of a shoulder,
the start of a smile and a fresh memory forms.

I become an accidental investigator of my own
home and its surrounds. At the supermarket,

I recognise an old neighbour. Initial words lead
to a brightened eye to the recounting of a story

it aids me to hear. It will change me in a way
that is irreversible. I smile at my empty hands.

Monostich XI: Redirections

I no longer speak over my own voice.

Pulling at the petals will not grow the flower.

True compliments don't arrive in words.

Unlearned: self-sacrifice.

It is time to disembark the bandwagon.

I turn the magnifying glass on myself.

In solitude, I am less alone.

Your daily schedule is a red herring.

I no longer trifle with my intuition.

Run toward what makes you tremble.

Avoidance

Another soft yet adamant thing
clambers to reach you, barred

by a cunning machinery assembled
by your own disruptive hand. Go,

work until you barely feel. Ascend
and trek physical instead of heart

distance; now, snap seeming beauty,
tackle yet another riddle external to

the partially opened one within. Go,
run from the wide-eyed initial version

of you. It's safe here, though see if
you do not falter, strangely, midway.

Behind every seeming journey's rise is a lock
to be picked. In a home, an abandoned room

with a window on the verge of collapse.
In that clumsy room is a call. Answer it.

Gone

A thing of the air came to me,
conversed and stayed willingly

for hours. Uncertain at times,
though returning and staying

a little longer each time. It's red
chest remained well-concealed,

it averted its gaze when I met it.
I felt its eyes on me when I moved

mine. One day it did not come.
I didn't feel alone before it visited,

but cannot return to how I was
after it. Now, I must learn how

to be solitary again; to imagine
I had never seen what I'd seen;

that I had not been rapidly woken,
wondering what the hidden parts

were, and whether the beauty would
have diminished with permanence.

Once More, Beginning

There is a glint of eye not yet finding
a translation into words; the opening

of trust; a trace of apprehension at the thought
of being injured again, yet a hint of the reason

you returned. Your voice spills over slightly
to again be reined in. You seem not to be

a creature reduced by pain, though you move
with a thin shade covering a bright filament.

See that your fear of being trapped again
does not create another trap. History repeats

only if we sidestep recognition. Here is a path
you have not walked, but you cannot travel it

shielded. Look unflinchingly at uncertainty.
Lay down the old reserve as I now seek to do.

Let's build a thing without bars, without trap
doors, without readying to flee before it begins.

As if life contained awareness of its brevity.
As though we accept, this time, we are free.

A Wish for You, Wherever You Are Now

You'll be rocked by a known arm in a warm room.
Neglect will not visit you early. There will be one,
maybe two, you'll meet who'll hear your silent call.
You'll not be afraid to utter the hard or the tender.
At the entry point of kinship, you will not falter:
you will guard it, recognise it swiftly, hold it fully.
In more instances than not, you will see entirely
what needs to be done and how, why and when.
You'll admit the smallest victories and realise
mistakes without severity or carelessness.
One ordinary day, I will pass you by.
As in the dream I had after you left,
you will be walking, decisive and smiling
in a town neither of us have yet set foot.
This time, I will need to catch your stride,
our paces switched in this new world.
You'll tell me your story without omission.

Monostich XII: Arrival

To the lavish room is a modest doorway.

The author of my alteration returns.

Misfit is my necessity.

The record is playing backward to reveal angels.

Despite your departure, we have no end.

I am my light keeper.

I walk down an unnamed street.

The fourth me is about to be born.

Notes

p.10, 'Monostitch II: Reversals': Trees 'laying their heads to the ground' refers to the way some trees in Siberia with shallow roots tilt and lean towards depression, due to thawing permafrost in the soil (caused by climate change).

The twisted train tracks refer to how hot temperatures can bend and warp train tracks, which is a current concern of the rail industry as temperatures warm.

p.56, 'Monostitch VI: Curiosities': Hajla is a traditional game Palestinian children play, similar to hopscotch.

Acknowledgements

A number of these poems have appeared (some in earlier forms) in the following publications:

Cordite Poetry Review, KalliopeX, Australian Poetry Anthology, Verity La, Live Encounters, Last Stanza Poetry Journal, Sweet Lit and *Rochford Street Review.*

'Change of Play' was shortlisted in the 2021 Hammond House Publishing International Literary Prize (UK) as Playground.

'Inside the Apartment' was Commended in the 2022 Melbourne Poets Union International Poetry Prize.

'Monostich VII: The Floods' was written as Poet in Residence/ Research Associate at the Monash Climate Change Communication Research Hub (Monash CliComm), 2022.

'Reef Tourist Boat', 'Monostich VIII: The Reef' and 'An Option' were written during a Neilma Sidney Literary Travel Grant from Writer's Victoria at the Great Barrier Reef, 2022.

I would like to acknowledge the Wurundjeri people of the Kulin Nation where I grew up, live and work and where the land was never ceded. Special thanks to Shane Strange at Recent Work Press for seeing something in this collection and Penelope Layland for her invaluable editorial advice. Much appreciation to Claire Gaskin and Robbie Coburn for their words of endorsement and poetic influence, Es Foong for their inspiration and support on many an occasion, and Ian McBryde for his mentorship and belief in me. I thank the staff at Readings and Joel Deane, Magan Magan, Manisha Anjali and Angela Costi for helping me launch the book and, of course, all those who unwittingly ended up inside a poem.

About the Author

Amanda Anastasi is a poet from Melbourne's west. Her poetry has appeared in *Australian Poetry Journal*, *The Massachusetts Review*, *Griffith Review*, *Cordite*, *Right Now* and *Best Australian Science Writing* 2021 and 2022.

Amanda has been the recipient of a Wheeler Centre Hot Desk Fellowship and was Poet in Resident for three years at the Monash Climate Change Communication Research Hub, tasked with communicating climate change and the 2019-2020 Australian bushfire crisis through poetry. Following this, she was the recipient of a Nielma Sidney Literary Travel Grant from Writer's Victoria to write poems at the Great Barrier Reef.

Amanda's previous collections are *2012 and other poems*, and *The Inheritors* (Black Pepper, 2021). She is also the convener of Melbourne's longest running poetry reading, La Mama Poetica.

9 780645 973280